ORANGUTAN

illustrated by Lynne Cherry

Methuen Children's Books

Orangutans live
in the thick green rain forest...

where they
swing...swing...
slowly through the treetops.

Wherever mother orangutan goes,
baby goes too.
Orangutans take good care
of their little ones.

Young orangutans play alone

or together.

It's raining in the forest.
The orangutans are dry
inside their nest.

for Julie Lee,
my good friend and fellow lover of forests

First published in Great Britain in 1987
by Methuen Children's Books Ltd
11 New Fetter Lane, London EC4P 4EE

Published in the United States by E P Dutton, New York
Text copyright © 1987 E P Dutton
Illustrations copyright © 1987 Lynne Cherry

Printed in Singapore by Tien Wah Press
All rights reserved
Licensed by World Wildlife Fund

ISBN 0 416 03012 2